NINETY-NINE NAMES OF
Love

expressions of the heart

NINETY-NINE NAMES of
Love

expressions of the heart

Priya Hemenway

Andrews McMeel
Publishing
Kansas City

To Jordan
& Saeidah...

Blessings on
you both,

Love
Cynthia,
Ken
& clan
2007

Book Design by Amy Ray

03 04 05 06 07 KFO 10 9 8 7 6 5 4 3 2 1

Library of Congress Cataloging-in-Publication Data

Hemenway, Priya
    Ninety-nine names of love: expressions of the heart/Priya Hemenway
      p. cm.
    ISBN: 0-7407-3831-3
    1. Man-woman relationships. 2. Love—Quotations, maxims, etc. 3. Love poetry. 4. Love—Religious aspects—Meditations. 5. Love—Miscellanea. I. Title: 99 names of love. II. Title: Love III. Title.

HQ801.A3H46 2003
306.7--dc21

                                                              2003048104

contents

Introduction

Love is like a rainbow with many colors and nuances—a prism through which we experience life and a treasure that grows richer with greater attention.

Like light, love is impossible to grasp, and like light it guides, perplexes, eludes, and mystifies us. In ways that are too numerous to contemplate, love sets a course for the divine, and whether we cooperate or not, love teaches its lessons and delivers the most wonderful surprises.

The many facets of love have long intrigued those who have journeyed within the inner dimensions, for love, like God, is indefinable. Love is the energy upon which we ride and the voice with which we pray when we journey to experience the essence of our being. As lover and beloved merge and become one, so do the seeker and the sought or the dancer and the dance. Within love we find union and the mystical state of ecstasy.

In the many religious traditions that have arisen in the world, love is the element that appears consistently and has the most universal understanding. While we may question the roles of the various faces of God or the dynamics of different dogmas, love is always recognized as the guiding emotion that serves human nature in living a spiritually fulfilled, healthy and happy life.

Whether we love one God or many, whether we live alone or with others, whether we practice prayer or meditation, it is the feelings in our hearts that help us discern right from wrong and thus guide us in our actions.

The seat of love is universally acknowledged to lie in the heart. Pumping blood into every nook and cranny of our body, it is an organ that is essential to life: No heart—no life. Surrounding the area of the heart as it sits in our chest, is the field or terrain of love. Contracting in times of pain or loss, this field can be rocky and full of deep pits of despair. Likewise, when love is felt, our chest opens up and feels expanded. Within the seat of love we walk on mountaintops and fly into the sky. As a part of the physical body the heart is extremely sensitive to the touch of others and to their attention. A loving thought from somewhere out of sight can evoke the same response in the heart as a loving glance from a few feet away.

Almost like a voice, the heart speaks to us from the depth of our being. A mouthpiece of the soul that so certainly, but elusively, resides within us, the heart is often perceived to be our closest connection to all that is mysterious and unknowable in life. The heart is, in fact, the incontrovertible proof that we are divine, for what use would the mouthpiece be if not to send a message that there is far more to life than is met by the body alone and far more to life than the mind can comprehend?

Through the heart we meet in love all aspects of life. Through the heart we hear the voices that describe life as it really is. Through the heart we touch what is eternal and sublime.

Ninety-Nine Names of Love are ninety-nine of the innumerable subtle aspects by which we recognize that life is divine. Love is awareness, love is compassion, love is understanding. Love has no limits in its ability to express the divine, for in love beauty is beheld, and God.

Ninety-Nine Names of Love are ninety-nine reflections upon the innumerable subtle aspects of love that have been given a voice by great poets and mystics who have always listened carefully to the messages of the heart.

Ninety-Nine Names of Love are ninety-nine subtle colors that make up the glorious rainbow that guides us to the treasures that lie within our soul. It is my hope that *Ninety-Nine Names of Love* will inspire you to explore the mystery that lies within.

ninety-nine names of
Love

Love is Awareness

You teach me to see things differently.

Reaching down through the ocean's foam

My fingers rest upon a pearl

At the bottom of the sea.

**HAKIM SANAI (TWELFTH CENTURY),
SUFI MYSTIC AND POET BORN IN AFGHANISTAN**

Love is a voice

The heart left,

And the friend is also gone.

I don't know whether I should go after the friend

or after the heart!

A voice spoke to me:

"Go in pursuit of the friend,

Because the lover needs a heart

In order to find union with the friend."

SHEIKH ABDULLAH ANSARI (1006–1089),
SUFI MASTER AND POET FROM AFGHANISTAN

Love is the present moment

The flower, the sky, your beloved,

can only be found in the present moment.

THICH NHAT HANH (1962–),
ZEN MASTER AND POET, BORN IN VIETNAM

Love is understanding

All, everything that I understand,
I understand only because I love.

LEO TOLSTOY (1828–1910),
RUSSIAN AUTHOR

love sees

with what eye do i see my beloved?

with his eye, not with mine,

for none sees him except himself.

IBN 'ARABI (1165–1240),
SUFI MYSTIC FROM SPAIN

Love Listens

In the sound of the ant's foot upon a rock

I hear you praised.

**HAKIM SANAI (TWELFTH CENTURY),
SUFI MYSTIC AND POET BORN IN AFGHANISTAN**

Love is calling

come, come, whoever you are,

wonderer, worshipper, lover of leaving,

ours is not a caravan of despair.

even if you have broken your vow a thousand times

it doesn't matter.

come, come, yet again, come, come.

JALALUDDIN RUMI (1207–1273),
SUFI MYSTIC AND POET BORN IN TAJIKISTAN

Love is Merging

Thy spirit is mingled in my spirit even as
wine is mingled with pure water.
When anything touches thee, it touches me.
Lo, in every case thou art I!

**MANSUR HALLAJ (B. 857),
SUFI MYSTIC AND MARTYR FROM SOUTHERN PERSIA**

love is god

i have seen my lord with the eye of my heart,

i said, "who are you?" he said, "you."

MANSUR HALLAJ (B. 857),
SUFI MYSTIC AND MARTYR FROM SOUTHERN PERSIA

LOVE is voiceless

o bird of the morning, learn love from the moth.

Because it burnt, lost its life, and said nothing.

SA'DI (1194–1292),
SUFI MYSTIC AND POET FROM PERSIA

Love is compassion

one thousand princes gathered and vowed to become buddhas. Avalokiteshvara promised to wait for his enlightenment until all the other princes had arrived.

for countless ages he devoted himself to this task. He
watched and waited while many attained enlightenment.
But for every one that attained, countless more entered the
realms of attachment, greed and bondage. seeing this
movement as an eternal situation, the prince was momen-
tarily overcome by grief and for a brief moment, lost faith.
At that moment his body exploded into one thousand
pieces.

calling out to all the Buddhas for help, he was immediate-
ly pieced back together. Repaired, his understanding deep-
ened and Avalokiteshvara rephrased his vow. He promised
to wait until every single soul was free—knowing this
would mean waiting forever.

TIBETAN STORY

love is a lamp

i am a lamp to thee who beholdest me,

i am a mirror to thee who perceivest me,

i am a door to thee who knockest at me,

i am a way to thee a wayfarer.

CHRISTIAN HYMN

Love is omniscient

To love is to know me,

My innermost nature,

The truth that I am.

**BHAGAVAD GITA: MYSTICAL INDIAN POEM
COMPOSED IN THE FIFTH CENTURY B.C.E.**

love is the protector

He who loves the world as his body
may be entrusted with the empire.

**LAO TZU (6TH CENTURY B.C.E.),
CHINESE MYSTIC**

Love is the guardian

I am fully qualified to work as a doorkeeper, for this
reason: what is inside me, I don't let out; what is
outside me, I don't let in. If someone comes in, he
goes right out again. He has nothing to do with me
at all. I am a doorkeeper of the heart,
not a lump of wet clay.

**RABI'A AL-'ADAWIYYA (717–801),
FEMALE SUFI MYSTIC BORN IN IRAQ**

Love is a Traveler

what you most want,

what you travel around

wishing to find,

lose, as lovers lose themselves,

and you will find.

**FARIDUDDIN 'ATTAR (1142–1220),
SUFI MYSTIC, CELEBRATED AS ONE OF
IRAN'S MOST PRESTIGIOUS POETS**

Love is Glorious

In that glory there is no "I" or "we" or "Thou."

"I," "we," "Thou," "He," and "she"

are all one thing.

MANSUR HALLAJ (B. 857),
SUFI MYSTIC AND MARTYR FROM SOUTHERN PERSIA

Love is the Beloved

In reality there is only the beloved, only loving.

MEHER BABA (1894–1969),
INDIAN SPIRITUAL MASTER AND PHILOSOPHER

Love is a craving

Your love has wrested me away from me,

you're the one I need, you're the one I crave.

Day and night I burn, gripped by agony,

you're the one I need, you're the one I crave.

YUNUS EMRE (1238–1320),
SUFI MYSTIC AND POET FROM TURKEY

Love is Ecstasy

All the bright-plumed birds of heaven

will devour their hearts with envy

in this place where we rest,

Thou and I.

It is the greatest wonder,

That we are sitting together here

in the same nook, at this moment,

Thou and I.

JALALUDDIN RUMI (1207–1273),
SUFI MYSTIC AND POET BORN IN TAJIKISTAN

Love is a conqueror

Love's conqueror is he whom love conquers.

**HAKIM SANAI (TWELFTH CENTURY),
SUFI MYSTIC AND POET BORN IN AFGHANISTAN**

LOVE is the friend

I set up house for you in my heart
As a friend that I could talk with.

**RABI'A AL-'ADAWIYYA (717–801),
FEMALE SUFI MYSTIC BORN IN IRAQ**

Love is a practice

piousness and the path of love
Are two different roads.
Love is the fire that burns
Both belief and nonbelief.
Those who practice love
Have neither religion nor caste.

**SHAIKH ABU SAEED ABIL KHEIR (967–1049),
SUFI MYSTIC AND POET**

love is pure

A wealthy man went to his garden, where his eye fell upon the beautiful wife of his gardener. He sent the man away and said to the woman, "shut the gates."

she replied, "I have shut them all except one, which I cannot shut."

He asked, "which one is that?"

"The gate," she said, "that is between us and god."

on receiving this answer, the man repented and begged to be forgiven.

SUFI TALE

Love is fearless

Love is fearlessness in the midst of the sea of fear.

JALALUDDIN RUMI (1207–1273),
SUFI MYSTIC AND POET BORN IN TAJIKISTAN

Love is a treasury

The heart is a treasury
in which god's mysteries are stored.

**LAHIJI (D. 1662),
PERSIAN PHILOSOPHER**

Love is Eternal

The whole world is a marketplace for love,

And nothing is excluded.

All things are made in love,

on love they all depend, to love all turn.

The earth, the heavens,

the sun, the moon, the stars—

The center of their orbit find in love.

**FARIDUDDIN 'ATTAR (1142–1220),
SUFI MYSTIC, CELEBRATED AS ONE OF
IRAN'S MOST PRESTIGIOUS POETS**

Love is incomparable

"whose beloved are you?" I asked,

"you who are so unbearably beautiful?"

"My own," he replied, "for I am one and alone

Love, lover, and beloved—

Mirror, beauty, eye."

**FAKHRUDDIN 'IRAQI (THIRTEENTH CENTURY),
SUFI MYSTIC AND MASTER OF LYRICS**

LOVE IS HIDDEN

close your eyes and try to catch him.

He is slipping by.

BAULS OF BENGAL,
WANDERING MYSTICS AND MINSTRELS IN INDIA

Love is a companion

Looking at my life I see that only love

Has been my soul's companion.

**JALALUDDIN RUMI (1207–1273),
SUFI MYSTIC AND POET BORN IN TAJIKISTAN**

Love is patience

Desirous to become a pupil of the famous sufi, Junayd of Baghdad, Shibli came to the master and said, "They tell me that you possess the pearl of divine knowledge: either give it me or sell it."

Junayd answered, "I cannot sell it, for you have not the price thereof; and if I give it you, you will have gained it cheaply. You do not know its value. Cast yourself headlong, like me, into this ocean of life in order that you may win the pearl by waiting patiently."

SUFI TALE

Love is a fire

o lamps of fire!

in whose splendors

the deep caverns of feeling,

once obscure and blind,

now give forth so exquisitely,

both warmth and light to their beloved.

ST. JOHN OF THE CROSS (1542–1591),
CHRISTIAN MYSTIC AND POET, BORN IN SPAIN

LOVE is the Rescuer

Beloved, show me the way out of this prison:

Erase from my mind all that is not you.

**ABU SA'ID IBN AB'IL KHAIR (967–1049),
SUFI MYSTIC AND POET FROM PERSIA**

Love is a Response

Never in the world does hatred cease by hatred;

Hatred ceases by love.

GAUTAMA BUDDHA (563–483 B.C.E.),
FOUNDER OF BUDDHISM

Love is Grateful

"The one sole wish of my heart," she replied,

"is still to be near thee, to sit by thy side;

To have thee by day in my happy sight,

And to lay my cheek on thy foot at night;

To lie in the shade of the cypress and sip

The sweet juice that lies on thy ruby lip;

To my wounded heart this soft balm to lay;

For naught beyond this can I wish or pray.

The streams of thy love will new life bestow on the

dry thirsty field where its sweet waters flow."

JAMI (1414–1492),
SUFI MYSTIC

Love is fulfilling

I hear bells ringing that no one has shaken,

inside love there is more joy than we know of,

Rain pours down, although the sky is clear of clouds,

There are whole rivers of light.

The universe is shot through in all parts

By a single sort of love.

How fulfilling is that joy in all our four bodies.

KABIR (1398–1518),
INDIAN MYSTIC AND POET

Love is Generous

Love is all we have,
The only way that each can help the other.

EURIPIDES (C. 480–406 B.C.),
POET OF ANCIENT GREECE

Love is Light

Love, like a flame, cannot fail to give out light.

**HAZRAT INAYAT KHAN (1882–1927),
SUFI MYSTIC AND TEACHER FROM INDIA**

Love Heals

When my friend is away from me I am depressed.

Nothing in the daylight delights me.

Sleep at night gives no rest.

Who can I tell about this?

The night is dark and long . . . hours go by . . .

Because I am alone, I sit up suddenly.

Fear goes through me . . .

Kabir says: listen my friend.

There is one thing in the world that satisfies,

And that is a meeting with the Beloved.

**KABIR (1398–1518),
INDIAN MYSTIC AND POET**

Love is Affectionate

The bride has entered

The sweet garden of her desire,

And she rests in delight,

Laying her neck

on the gentle arms of her Beloved.

**ST. JOHN OF THE CROSS (1542–1591),
CHRISTIAN MYSTIC AND POET, BORN IN SPAIN**

LOVE is Desire

He cannot glance away without glancing back,

His desire rekindled.

**FAKHRUDDIN 'IRAQI (THIRTEENTH CENTURY),
SUFI MYSTIC AND MASTER OF LYRICS**

Love is surrender

from deep inside, love cries out:

Do not wait, surrender for the sake of love.

JALALUDDIN RUMI (1207–1273),
SUFI MYSTIC AND POET BORN IN TAJIKISTAN

Love is a Reward

Caliph Harun al-Rashid's favorite concubine was very plain, but he preferred her to all of her beautiful rivals. When asked for a reason, the caliph offered a simple demonstration.

He summoned all his concubines and then opened the door of his private treasure chamber, which was filled with gold and jewels. He told the women that they could take whatever they desired. They all ran to gather up as much as they could, except his favorite, who did not even enter the treasure chamber.

"Why don't you take something for yourself?" asked the caliph.

The woman replied, "All I want is to serve you. You are all that I need. You are the one I love, and your love is all the reward I want."

SUFI TALE

Love prevails

Those who adapt themselves
will be preserved until the end.

That which bends can be straightened.
That which is empty can be filled.
That which is worn away can be renewed.

**LAO TZU (6TH CENTURY B.C.E.),
CHINESE MYSTIC**

LOVE IS TRUE

True love knows no after-thoughts;

with love, good and evil cease to exist.

**FARIDUDDIN 'ATTAR (1142–1220),
SUFI MYSTIC, CELEBRATED AS ONE OF
IRAN'S MOST PRESTIGIOUS POETS**

Love is intimacy

where is intimacy found
if not in the give and take of love.

**JALALUDDIN RUMI (1207–1273),
SUFI MYSTIC AND POET BORN IN TAJIKISTAN**

LOVE IS DELIGHT

Two sages had taken up the topic of love.

One declared: "The hallmarks of love are misfortune and suffering. Incessantly the lover experiences torment and affliction."

The other replied, "Enough! I suppose you have never seen peace follow war, or tasted the joy of union after separation! None in the world are more delightful than those who, with a pure heart, give themselves to love; and none cruder than those insensitive beings who remain aloof from such cares!"

JAMI (1414–1492),
SUFI MYSTIC AND POET

Love is unity

A girl fell in a river—in a flash
Her lover dived in with a mighty splash,
And fought the current till he reached her side.
When they were safe again, the poor girl cried:
"By chance I tumbled in, but why should you
come after me and hazard your life too?"
He said: "I dived because the difference
of 'I' and 'you' to lovers makes no sense—
A long time passed when we were separate,
But now that we have reached this single state
when you are me, and I am wholly you,
what use is it to talk of us as two?"

FARIDUDDIN 'ATTAR (1142–1220),
SUFI MYSTIC AND POET

Love is Attraction

Not only the thirsty seek the water,

The water as well seeks the thirsty.

**JALALUDDIN RUMI (1207–1273),
SUFI MYSTIC AND POET BORN IN TAJIKISTAN**

Love is freedom

I speak frankly and that makes me happy:
I am the slave of love, I am free of both worlds.

**HAFIZ OF SHIRAZ (1230–1291),
THE GREATEST LYRIC POET OF PERSIA**

Love is perfect

Indulge me a moment while I sit by your side.

without a glimpse of your face,

my heart cannot rest,

And my work becomes drudgery

in an endless sea of toil.

Today summer came to my window,

signing and murmuring,

And the bees played like minstrels

At the court of flowery groves.

Now we'll sit quietly, each to each,

And sing our dedication to life

In silent and ever-flowing ease.

**RABINDRANATH TAGORE (1861–1941),
ONE OF MODERN INDIA'S GREATEST POETS**

Love cannot be understood

You are as wide as the world and sky

Your feet go deeper than the abyss

And deeper still!

Your crown stands high above the universe

And higher still!

You are imperceptible, past understanding

unlimited and incomparable.

**BASAVANNA (1131–1167),
HINDU SAINT AND SOCIAL REFORMER**

Love is a Dance

This sky where we live

is no place to lose your wings,

so love, love, love.

HAFIZ OF SHIRAZ (1230–1291),
THE GREATEST LYRIC POET OF PERSIA

LOVE is a connoisseur

only a connoisseur of the flavors of love

can comprehend the language of a lover's heart.

others have no clue.

**BAULS OF BENGAL,
WANDERING MYSTICS AND MINSTRELS IN INDIA**

Love is a Mirror

I am he whom I love, and he whom I love is I.

we are two spirits dwelling in one body.

if thou seest me, thou seest him;

And if thou seest him, thou seest us both.

MANSUR HALLAJ (B. 857),
SUFI MYSTIC AND MARTYR FROM SOUTHERN PERSIA

Love is a comfort

To abandon all that he has fashioned

And hold in the palm of my hand

The simple proof that he loves me—

That is the goal of my search.

**RABI'A AL-'ADAWIYYA (717–801),
FEMALE SUFI MYSTIC BORN IN IRAQ**

Love is complete

Love arrives complete,
Just like the moon in the window.

**JALALUDDIN RUMI (1207–1273),
SUFI MYSTIC AND POET BORN IN TAJIKISTAN**

love is a revelation

knowing nothing shuts the iron gates;

a fresh love opens them.

KABIR (1398–1518),
INDIAN MYSTIC AND POET

Love is an Echo

Sight is not the only way that love enters the heart;
It often happens that love is born of the spoken word.
The echo of beauty entering the ear
May rob heart and soul of peace and reason.

**JAMI (1414–1492),
SUFI MYSTIC**

Love is Beauty

If love manifests itself within you,

It has its origins in beauty.

You are nothing but a mirror

In which beauty is reflected.

JAMI (1414–1492),
SUFI MYSTIC

Love is fantastic

Kabir says: fantastic!

Don't let a chance like this go by!

KABIR (1398–1518),
INDIAN MYSTIC AND POET

love is clarity

Hidden meanings abound as my sight becomes clear.

HAKIM SANAI (TWELFTH CENTURY),
SUFI MYSTIC AND POET BORN IN AFGHANISTAN

LOVE IS CHAOS

He then raised his parasol and hoisted his banners

To mingle being and nothingness.

Ah, the chaos of enraptured love

Has thrown the world in tumult!

**FAKHRUDDIN 'IRAQI (THIRTEENTH CENTURY),
SUFI MYSTIC AND MASTER OF LYRICS**

Love is a Drunkard

come, let's scatter roses and pour wine in the glass;

we'll shatter heaven's roof and lay a new foundation.

if sorrow raises armies to shed the blood of lovers,

let's join with the wine bearer and overthrow them!

with a string at hand, play a song, my friend,

let's clap and sing a song and lose our heads in dancing.

HAFIZ OF SHIRAZ (1230–1291),
THE GREATEST LYRIC POET OF PERSIA

LOVE is a guest

The beloved of my heart is the guest of my soul.

RABI'A AL-'ADAWIYYA (717–801),
FEMALE SUFI MYSTIC BORN IN IRAQ

Love is passion

with passion pray. with passion make love.

with passion eat and drink and dance and play.

why swim like a dead fish in this ocean of love?

**JALALUDDIN RUMI (1207–1273),
SUFI MYSTIC AND POET BORN IN TAJIKISTAN**

love is present

why is there always music in this house?

ask the owner.

come in.

The beloved is here.

we are all drunk and no one notices

who enters or leaves.

Don't sit outside the door in the dark.

JALALUDDIN RUMI (1207–1273),
SUFI MYSTIC AND POET BORN IN TAJIKISTAN

Love is sacrifice

Raqqam, Nuri, and some other sufis had been accused of heresy and were sentenced to death. when the executioner approached Raqqam, Nuri rose and offered himself in his friend's place with the utmost cheerfulness and submission. All the spectators were astounded.

The executioner said, "Young man, the sword is not a thing that people are so eager to meet; and your turn has not yet arrived."

Nuri answered, "Life is the most precious thing in the world: I wish to sacrifice for my friend's sake the few moments which remain."

SUFI TALE

Love is an ocean

As the tide comes in we caress each other.

when it withdraws, I drop to his feet in prayer.

KAHLIL GIBRAN (1883–1931),
POET, PHILOSOPHER, AND ARTIST, BORN IN LEBANON

Love is silence

Love, silent as the night,

Not one word will you say . . .

JACOPONE DA TODI (1230–1306),
ITALIAN RELIGIOUS POET

Love is All-consuming

A man once fell madly in love with a beautiful woman. He followed her for days and finally went up to her on the street and declared his undying, all-consuming love.

He went on and on, and finally the woman interrupted, "Your words are lovely, but my sister is coming along behind me. She is far more beautiful than I am, and I'm sure that you will prefer her to me."

As the man spun around to look at the beautiful sister, the woman slapped him sharply on the back of his neck. She exclaimed, "I thought you said that your love for me was all-consuming and undying. Some love you have! The instant I mentioned a more beautiful woman, you turned away from me to look at her. You don't even know the meaning of love!"

SUFI TALE

LOVE IS DEATH

strange is the path
when you pursue love.
your body is crushed at the first step.

If you want to taste love
be prepared to cut off your head
And sit on it.

MIRABAI (1498–1550),
FEMALE INDIAN POET

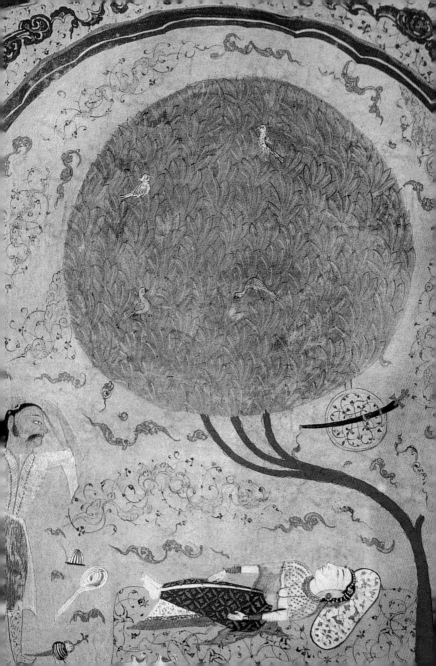

Love is a cure

The source of my suffering is deep in my heart.

It is a disease no doctor can cure.

Only in union with the beloved will it cease.

RABI'A AL-'ADAWIYYA (717–801),
FEMALE SUFI MYSTIC BORN IN IRAQ

Love is Energy

He is the inmost self of all. Fire—his head; sun and moon—his eyes; the four quarters—his ears; revelation—his voice; wind—his breath; world—his heart; earth—his feet.

MUNDAKA UPANISHAD,
HINDU SCRIPTURE

Love is Breathing

o you who have departed from your own self,

And who have not yet

Reached the friend:

Be not sad,

For love accompanies you in every breath.

**SHEIKH ABDULLAH ANSARI (1006–1089),
SUFI MASTER AND POET FROM AFGHANISTAN**

love is a secret

Now will I draw aside the veil,

And in the temple of mine inmost soul

Behold the friend, incomparable love.

He who would know the secret of both worlds

will find that the secret of them both is love.

FARIDUDDIN 'ATTAR (1142–1220),
SUFI MYSTIC

Love is Aloneness

My peace is in my aloneness.

My beloved is alone with me there, always.

**RABI'A AL-'ADAWIYYA (717–801),
FEMALE SUFI MYSTIC BORN IN IRAQ**

Love is inspiration

My soul gave my heart a brilliant idea.

HAFIZ OF SHIRAZ (1230–1291),
THE GREATEST LYRIC POET OF PERSIA

Love is strong

Those who don't feel this love

pulling them like a river,

Those who don't drink dawn

Like a cup of spring water

or take in sunset like supper,

Those who don't want to change,

Let them sleep.

**JALALUDDIN RUMI (1207–1273),
SUFI MYSTIC AND POET BORN IN TAJIKISTAN**

Love is painful

Last night I strutted about like a peacock
in the garden of union
But today, through separation from my friend,
I twist my head like a snake.
The profit of the sea would be good
if there were no fear of waves.
The company of the rose would be sweet
if there were no pain from thorns.

SA'DI (1194–1292),
SUFI MYSTIC AND POET FROM PERSIA

Love is Ingenious

Love the beautician

mixes her cosmetics

turning truth into a metaphor.

**FAKHRUDDIN 'IRAQI (THIRTEENTH CENTURY),
SUFI MYSTIC AND MASTER OF LYRICS**

Love is the seen

one who pervades the great universe
is seen by none, unless that one knows
the unfolding of love.

**CHANDIDAS (FIFTEENTH CENTURY),
HIGH PRIEST REBEL-POET OF BENGAL**

Love is inescapable

Fetter me! Bind me! Lock me in the jail
of thy delicious arms; make fast around me
The silk-soft manacles of wrists and hands,
Then kill me! I shall never break those bands.

**GITA GOVINDA (EARLY TWELFTH CENTURY),
INDIAN LYRICAL POEM**

Love is Emptiness

Go sweep out the chamber of your heart,

Make it ready to be

The dwelling place of the beloved,

When you depart, she will enter,

In that void she will display her beauty.

MAHMUD SHABISTARI (1250–1320),
CELEBRATED AUTHOR OF SUFISM

love is the sought

what do all seek so earnestly? 'tis love.

what do they whisper to each other? love.

FARIDUDDIN 'ATTAR (1142–1220),
SUFI MYSTIC

Love is union

union is yours when this dream-world
fades and dies away.

**MAHMUD SHABISTARI (1250–1320),
CELEBRATED AUTHOR OF SUFISM**

LOVE IS JOY

My beloved speaks and says to me,

"Arise, my love, my fair one, and come away;

For lo, the winter is past,

The rain is over and gone.

The flowers appear on the earth;

The time of singing has come,

And the voice of the turtledove is heard in our land.

The fig tree puts forth its figs,

And the vines are in blossom;

They give forth fragrance,

Arise, my love, my fair one, and come away."

SONG OF SOLOMON, BIBLE

Love is a Garden

Do not go to the garden of flowers!

O friend! go not there;

In your body is the garden of flowers.

Take your seat on the thousand petals of the lotus,

and there gaze on the infinite beauty.

KABIR (1398–1518),
INDIAN MYSTIC AND POET

Love is uncertainty

I follow the religion of love:

whatever way love's camels take,

That is my religion and my faith.

**IBN 'ARABI (1165–1240),
SUFI MYSTIC FROM SPAIN**

Love is Beneficence

He came to my house and asked for charity.

And I fell on my knees and cried,

"Beloved, what may I give?"

"Just love," he said. "Just love."

ST. FRANCIS OF ASSISI (C. 1181–1226),
FOUNDER OF THE ORDER OF FRANCISCAN MONKS,
PATRON SAINT OF ANIMALS AND ECOLOGY

Love is the Beginning

Darkness there was: at first concealed in darkness,

All was indiscriminated chaos.

All that existed then was void and formless.

Then, in the beginning, desire arose.

Desire, the primal seed and germ of spirit.

RIG-VEDA,
OLDEST OF THE FOUR HINDU SCRIPTURES CALLED VEDAS

love is a seduction

How can I describe his relentless flute,

which pulls virtuous women from their homes

And drags them by their hair to shyam

As thirst and hunger pull the doe to the snare?

chaste ladies forget their lords,

wise men forget their wisdom,

And clinging vines shake loose from their trees,

Hearing that music.

**CHANDIDASA (15TH CENTURY),
INDIAN POET**

Love is a veil

"I" and "you" are but the lattices,
in the niches of a lamp,
Through which the one light shines.

**MAHMUD SHABISTARI (1250–1320),
CELEBRATED AUTHOR OF SUFISM**

LOVE is Life

If you want to live, die in love;

Die in love if you want to remain alive.

JALALUDDIN RUMI (1207–1273),
SUFI MYSTIC AND POET BORN IN TAJIKISTAN

love is everywhere

His hands and feet are everywhere, he has heads and mouths everywhere: he sees all, he hears all. He is in all and he is. He is the wandering swan everlasting, the soul of all in the universe, the spirit of fire in the ocean of life. To know him is to overcome death, and he is the only path to life eternal.

SVETASVATURA UPANISHAD,
HINDU SCRIPTURE

Love is worthy

I have two ways of loving you:

A selfish one

And another way that is more worthy of you.

In my selfish love,

I remember you and you alone.

In that other love,

You lift the veil

And let me feast my eyes on your living face.

**RABI'A AL-'ADAWIYYA (717–801),
FEMALE SUFI MYSTIC BORN IN IRAQ**

love is difficult

o saki, bring around the cup of wine and offer it to me,

for love seemed easy at first, but then grew difficult.

HAFIZ OF SHIRAZ (1230–1291),
THE GREATEST LYRIC POET OF PERSIA

Love is Truth

Reason is powerless in the expression of Love
for love alone is capable of revealing the truth.

JALALUDDIN RUMI (1207–1273),
SUFI MYSTIC AND POET BORN IN TAJIKISTAN

Love is Right

Sultan Mahmud possessed many slaves, each of whom was a marvel of beauty. The sultan was asked how it happened that he manifested towards none of them so much attention and love as to Iyaz, who was much less handsome than the others.

He replied: "whatever descends into the heart appears good to the eye."

SUFI TALE

Acknowledgments

Cover, page 80: Collection of Villiers David, London.

Pages 14, 53, 71: National Museum, New Delhi.

Pages 17, 68, 74: Bharat Kala Bhavan, Varanasi.

Pages 20, 39, 47, 116: Ehrenfeld Collection, San Francisco.

Pages 23, 107: Metropolitan Museum of Art, New York.

Pages 26, 101: Museum of Fine Arts, Boston.

Pages 29, 98, 110, 137: British Library, London.

Page 32, 149: Collection of Gopi Krishna Kanoria, Patna.

Pages 35, 44, 62, 143: British Museum, London.

Pages 40, 119, 122: Bodleian Library, Oxford.

Page 50: Keir Collection, Ham, England.

Page 56: Heydt Museum, Wuppertal.

Page 59: Collection of Valentine Chagall, Saint-Paul-de-Vence, France.

Page 65: Sri Pratap Singh Museum, Srinagar.

Pages 77, 152: Jagdish and Kimla Mittal Museum of Indian Art, Hyderabad.

Page 83, 113: The Chester Beatty Library, Dublin.

Page 86: Corbis, London.

Page 89: Government Museum and Art Gallery, Chandigarh.

Page 92: Collection of H. Peter Stern, Mountainville, N.Y.

Page 95: Collection of Stedelijk Museum, Amsterdam.

Pages 104, 134: Asutosh Museum of Indian Art, University of Calcutta, India.

Page 125: Prince of Wales Museum, Bombay.

Page 128: © Chakrabhand Posayakrit.

Pages 131, 146: Freer Gallery of Art, Smithsonian Institution, Washington, DC.

Page 140: The Russian Museum, Leningrad.

Page 155: Alvin O. Bellak Collection, Philadelphia.

Page 158: State Museum, Lucknow.